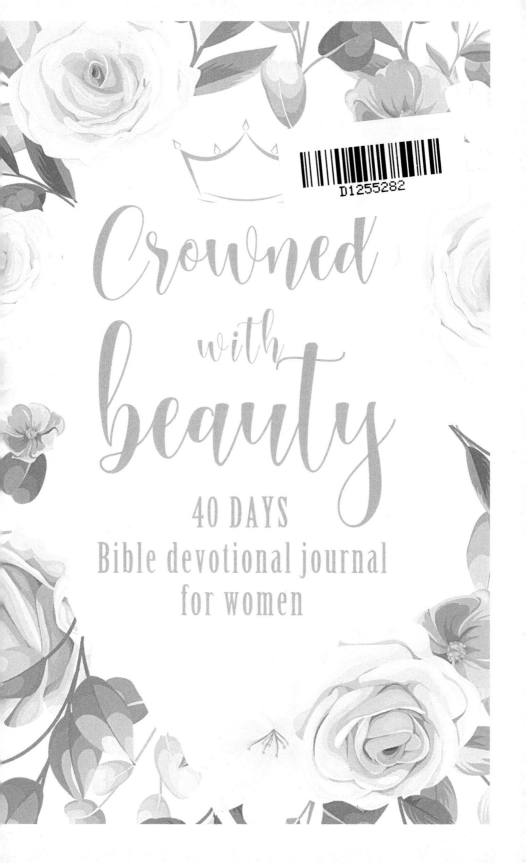

Crowned with beauty

40 DAYS
Bible devotional journal
for women

All Scriptures are taken from the NIV translation of the Bible
Josanne Anthony, D.Min. P.M.Bogdan
Living His Story Designs

YOU SHALL BE A

crown of beauty

IN THE HAND OF THE LORD, AND THE

royal diadem

IN THE HAND OF YOUR GOD

Isa.62:2

Introduction

Prayer is a powerful weapon.

While it simply means to communicate with God, the depths of prayer are far reaching.

Praying connects us with our Maker, the One who loves us beyond our greatest imagination. It keeps a line of communication open with the One who is perfecting us. It gives us the opportunity to exercise and grow our mustard seed-sized faith.

Prayer can reach our loved ones when we can't. It can encourage the discouraged, bring healing to those who are sick, and even work miracles in impossible situations.

We invite you to use this prayer journal during your daily time of devotion with the Lord. Each day shares a scripture and thought that relates to it, concluding with thought provoking questions and suggestions for action. Each day is different and is intended to explore many different areas of your life, whether for yourself inwardly, or for people are situations around you.

Let the pages of this journal dig deep inside of you. Let them challenge you. Allow the scriptures and thoughts to expose hidden secrets and untold shortcomings. Become completely transparent before the Lord.

Acknowledge your need for growth in certain areas. Let your weaknesses and deficiencies rest in the hands of the Master Potter that will mold you into a perfect masterpiece like no other!

Let the pages of this journal remind you of the needs surrounding you through family, friends and acquaintances. You will find prompts to reach out to others that need to know someone cares. You may find that the prayers you offered for loved ones is the prayer that changed their lives!

As a bonus, at the end of the journal we added five coloring pages with the Scriptures from the journal.

Are you ready to dig deeper within your soul and draw closer to your Creator? Here's a guarantee: if you will allow this journal to challenge you, you will not finish it the same way you started.

Be blessed, be challenged, be changed!

- Day 1 -

Do not be anxious about anything, but in every situation, by prayer and petition, with thanksgiving, present your requests to God. And the peace of God, which transcends all understanding, will guard your hearts and your minds in Christ Jesus.

Philippians 4:6-7

Life gives us plenty of choice topics when anxiety wants to invade our personal space: marriage, children, job situations, finances, and more.
Jesus said He came to give us life more abundantly, not life with more anxiety.
When our life is in His hands, we can trust Him to move on the petitions we give to Him.

Remember that worry offers no reward, but the prayer of the righteous is powerful and effective.
List loved ones, friends and situations that will benefit from your prayers..

- Day 2 -

I can do all this through him who gives me strength.

Philippians 4:13

Seasons in life vary like the seasons in nature. Sometimes things are beautiful, warm and joyful, while other times things are messy, cold and miserable.
When we rely on the strength of Jesus instead of our own power, we can endure all things..

Do you remember a difficult season you went through that you are confident it was God's strength that carried you through? Write your feelings of gratitude about how He helped you.

- Day 3 -

Rejoice in the Lord always. I will say it again: Rejoice!

Philippians 4:4

Delighting in Jesus on our Christian journey prevents wrong attitudes when life is challenging. Keeping the blessing of redemption in the forefront of our minds will always trump a bad day that tempts us to complain.

List five to ten reasons you have to be thankful as a Christian. What blessings do you have that wouldn't be possible without the hand of God in your life?

- Day 4 -

Give thanks to the LORD, for he is good. His love endures forever.

Psalm 136:1

We all have days when our emotions feel distorted and our actions are less than desirable. Isn't it good to know that God loves us regardless? How good it is to have His faithful love, and how encouraging to know He will let us try again tomorrow.

Don't write down your shortcomings of today, but instead write down your hopes and intentions for tomorrow. Think of what you can do to help tomorrow be better.

- Day 5 -

Trust in the LORD with all your heart and lean not on your own understanding; in all your ways submit to him, and he will make your paths straight.

Psalm 136:1

Submission can sometimes be interchangeable with trusting because we're completely turning over the reins of our hearts to Jesus.
What great assurance when leading is done by the Lord. All we need to do is follow.

Do you struggle with fully submitting to the will and ways of God? What do you think hinders your complete trust? What will help you to completely surrender to God?

- Day 6 -

Come to me, all you who are weary and burdened, and I will give you rest.

Matthew 11:28

Sometimes we just need someone to talk to: someone to just listen on the days our minds feel frazzled, our worries seem endless and our responsibilities too many. A good, long talk with Jesus brings rest and renewed strength to pull ourselves back together.

Have you taken the time lately to just talk to Jesus as your best Friend? He's listening. Spend some time sharing your world with Him. He already knows and doesn't need you to tell Him, but you need you to talk to Him.

- Day 7 -

A cheerful heart is good medicine, but
a crushed spirit dries up the bones.

Proverbs 17:22

A happy and optimistic attitude really is good medicine. It combats stress and pain, protects the heart, lowers blood pressure and more. A depressed and pessimistic lifestyle is not God's will for us.

Spend today reminiscing on all the ways God has moved in your life. Spend some time naming the blessings that surround you. Consider the things you can omit from your life that hinder you spiritually.

– Day 8 –

Above all, love each other deeply, because love covers over a multitude of sins.

1 Peter 4:8

 Isn't it a relief that our God who knows our deepest struggles, ugliest attitudes, darkest sins and irrational fears does not shout them from the heavens, for all the world to know? That is how we should react to the flaws and weaknesses of those we love.
If we truly love, forgiveness and restoration should be our goal.

Do you know anyone who is struggling with ongoing sin in their lives? Pray for that person today. Furthermore, encourage her and let her know you love her.

- Day 9 -

For where your treasure is, there your heart will be also.

Matthew 6:21

We can lay up our treasures with material things that give only temporary satisfaction. Cars wear out, fashion changes, and mansions aren't much without love.
The better choices are the treasures accumulated through the heart-things like love, compassion and kindness. Those things carry on through the generations and are much more rewarding.

Is your heart focused on the right treasures? How can you add to them today?

- Day 10 -

A wife of noble character who can find? She is worth far more than rubies.

Proverbs 31:10

It can be intimidating when we compare ourselves to other women, married or single. There will always be others who are more physically attractive or whose homes are more beautiful or who earn more money than we do. But more valuable than any of those things is the woman who is honorable. That is something all of us can acquire.

Have you given yourself a fair evaluation when you look at yourself? Or are you your greatest, unfair critic?   Write down ten positive things about your character and begin to see your worth, if you haven't already.

- Day 11 -

Peace I leave with you; my peace I give you. I
do not give to you as the world gives. Do not let
your hearts be troubled and do not be afraid.

John 14:27

 The world offers solutions to finding peace
through many means: dancing, creating,
talking and more. However, Jesus offers true
peace, and that is found through a pure
conscience that is right with our Savior.
Other ideas are simply bandages and not
a cure.

Is there anything in your life that is
hindering your peace? Are there things you
need to talk to the Savior about? He's ready
when you are.

- Day 12 -

Cast your cares on the LORD and he will sustain you; he will never let the righteous be shaken.

Psalm 55:22

Taking our cares to our neighbors, siblings, children or others may bring temporary relief to what we are facing. Even so, none of them offer the strength and stability we need when we're faced with uncertainties. Taking our cares to Jesus gives Him the opportunity to give us the grace we need to always stand.

When you pray and the words don't come, just cry. Stay in the presence of the Lord and let Him soothe you. Don't be in a hurry. He hears you in silent times too.

- Day 13 -

In the same way, the Spirit helps us in our weakness. We do not know what we ought to pray for, but the Spirit himself intercedes for us through wordless groans.

Romans 8:26

When there are no words to describe the aching in our hearts, or we see a need but can't see a solution, it's ok. God knows how to interpret our burdens, our tears and our inability to describe how we feel. We can go ahead and cry. The tears and time without words are never wasted.

When you pray and the words don't come, just cry. Stay in the presence of the Lord and let Him soothe you. Don't be in a hurry. He hears you in silent times too.

- Day 14 -

Therefore, if anyone is in Christ, he is a new creation. The old has passed away; behold, the new has come.

2 Corinthians 5:17

Being new creation is a gift beyond measure! Having a fresh start by walking with Jesus allows us to leave our past mistakes behind. God offers mercy, and we need to accept it along with forgiving ourselves. Dwelling on past mistakes hinders the future of what God wants to do in us.

Are you holding on to the feelings of defeat from your past? Acknowledge those feelings and consider the ways that they can hinder you. Talk to Jesus and ask for His help in completely releasing those feelings, so that you can be the new creation He desires you to be.

- Day 15 -

Therefore encourage one another and build each other up, just as in fact you are doing.

1 Thessalonians 5:11

Friends that generously give words of encouragement to us in different situations are the ones who help us to make it over obstacles and challenges in our lives. Someone who casts their vote of confidence in our abilities to thrive can be the voice we needed for that extra boost to keep going.

Are you a voice that lifts up the fallen or weak? Do you offer those few little words that someone needed to go a little further? Take a moment to thank God for those whose words have made the difference for you. Ask the Lord to give you the right words to make a difference for others.

- Day 16 -

Listen to advice and accept discipline, and at the end you will be counted among the wise.

Proverbs 19:20

We must never allow ourselves to be offended when advice is being given to us. People offer a mixture of wisdom from different generations and experiences. There is no shame in not knowing it all.
Accept good advice. Be humble when we are disciplined. It may sting a little when given but will bless us if we heed to it.

Have you been struggling with accepting advice from others? Has verbal correction come to you? Pray for the Lord to protect your spirit from any pride that would hinder your recognition to error, or the need for growth.

- Day 17 -

I thank my God every time I remember you. In all my prayers for all of you, I always pray with joy...

Philippians 1:3-4

A walk down memory lane reminds us of the many different people who have poured into our lives. Family members, neighbors, friends, pastors and church families have played a role in many of our lives to contribute to who we are today.
Gratitude for these special people should have a permanent place in our hearts.

Who has impacted your life and your walk? Spend some time naming each one and pray for them individually. Return some encouragement to them by sending a card expressing your gratitude to them.

- Day 18 -

Pray continually...

1 Thessalonians 5:17

Prayer is not only the times where we quietly make our exit to spend an hour talking with our Lord. It also includes those many, many moments throughout each day when feelings of gratitude rise up for something we've seen, or the memory of an answered prayer comes to mind. It is those times when we take a concern to the Lord, or we ask Him to help someone we see struggling through their day. Prayer is simply communicating with God. He's always listening, and He loves to hear our voices.

List ten different things you can share with the Lord today. Extend your personal prayer time into a conversation with your best Friend that is sprinkled throughout your day.

- Day 19 -

So do not fear, for I am with you; do not be dismayed, for I am your God. I will strengthen you and help you; I will uphold you with my righteous right hand.

Isaiah 41:10

The emotions of women are many, and because we care so deeply, anxieties and fears become our unwanted companions too often. It isn't intentional that we allow ourselves to be consumed with worry at times. Even so, we must remind ourselves that Jesus is our strength! He is with us! He will help us through!

Are there worries that are trying to consume you right now? Write them down. Once they are penned out, take them to the Lord, and leave them there. Ask His help with releasing fear and learning to trust Him completely.

- Day 20 -

Take delight in the LORD, and he will give you the desires of your heart.

Psalm 37:4

How we assess our walk with the Lord will produce following results naturally. If we consider this journey drudgery or an obligation, our heart will be on the world and its offerings. But if we love our journey and face each day of living for God with joy, our hearts will be filled with the things He wants us to have.

Make a list of the things you find yourself desiring in your life right now. Are they Godly desires, or worldly desires? Your list may surprise you, and if it does, that is a good thing.
Sometimes we don't realize that our love is growing cold. This is a perfect opportunity to re-focus your desires.

- Day 21 -

If any of you lacks wisdom, you should ask God, who gives generously to all without finding fault, and it will be given to you.

James 1:5

Do we ever stop and think that God may be watching us, and that He is waiting for that glorious moment when we ask Him to give us wisdom? Situations are many, and with each passing year, the world in general faces more complex issues than the year before. He looks forward to imparting wisdom to us. He knows we need it, and it must please Him when we realize we need it.

What areas do you feel are most pressing in your need for wisdom? Write them down. While the Lord will bring situations to help you grow in wisdom, search the scriptures on each subject to let God teach you from His Word as well.

- Day 22 -

I praise you because I am fearfully and wonderfully made; your works are wonderful, I know that full well.

Psalm 139:14

It's amazing how our insecurities can follow us past childhood and throughout our adult lives. Comments about our appearance or our strong character traits can vex us for years. For those of us who question our own value, no matter our age, let's lay aside that unnecessary weight today.

What character traits have been cast negatively about yourself from others? Write them down and consider how those traits can be used by God.

- Day 23 -

The tongue has the power of life and death, and those who love it will eat its fruit.

Proverbs 18:21

  To think that a formed sound we release from our mouths can completely transform another person is nothing less than astounding. Whether for the positive of the negative, our words matter. A lot.
Be one whose love for power in the tongue is life!

Who do you know that needs to hear words of life today? What can you say to breath hope into them? What scriptures do you want to encourage them with?

- Day 24 -

What good will it be for someone to gain the whole world, yet forfeit their soul? Or what can anyone give in exchange for their soul?

Proverbs 18:21

   The world will always try to entice us to follow its shallow happiness. It offers material things in exchange for true peace and joy found in a relationship with our Savior. We have no reason to be intimidated or tempted by promises of greatness offered by the world. A modest life serving the Lord is more precious than any prize given in exchange.

Have feelings of inadequacy been taunting your soul to have greater things? Talk to the Lord about them. Weed out the ones that bring no true value. Let His Spirit remind you of what the priceless things you already possess.

- Day 25 -

One thing I ask from the Lord, this only do I seek: that I may dwell in the house of the Lord all the days of my life, to gaze on the beauty of the Lord and to seek him in his temple.

Psalm 27:4

Times will come when life is overwhelming, discouraging and confusing. No matter what comes our way, let us hold fast to our devotion to God. Let us do all we can to make it to His house and to worship and seek after Him. Problems will pass. Jesus will always stay, and will even walk with us through the hard times.

Have you been struggling to make it to the house of the Lord? Write down the reasons why. Recognize God's ability to deliver, encourage and strengthen you. Commit to be in His house when the doors open again.

- Day 26 -

A friend loves at all times, and a brother is born for a time of adversity.

Proverbs 17:17

It's easy to feel all alone, even in a world of over seven billion people. But oh, aren't we thankful for true friends? Isn't it a blessing to know who we can count on when we need someone to talk to, or a shoulder to cry on? True friends are one of the greatest treasures in life!

Ponder on the amazing variety of friends the Lord has blessed you with. Some will encourage you, challenge you, admonish you, and above all, love you.
Make a list of those who are always there for you. Pray that the Lord will bless them in a special way today.

- Day 27 -

Rejoice with those who rejoice; mourn with those who mourn.

Romans 12:15

The people we love and feel the closest to walk through many situations that stir up many different emotions, just like us. Sharing in their joy makes their experience even sweeter. When their hearts are aching, simply being there to mourn with them helps tremendously. We don't need to worry if we don't have the right words. We just need to show we care.

Is there someone you can express your happiness for today? Is there someone you've avoided because you haven't known what to say about what they are going through? Make a note to call them today. Let them know you care.

- Day 28 -

She gets up while it is still night; she provides food for her family and portions for her female servants.

Proverbs 31:15

This ideal woman, described in Proverbs, got her plate full. Some of us understand, and some of us are past this particular stage of life. Regardless, life keeps all of us busy. On the days we fail to do it all, remember that tomorrow is a new day to try again. On the days we conquer our to-do lists, let us remember to thank God for the grace to get it all done.

If your family is grown, you may be past the stage of planning big meals round-the-clock. Even so, pray for your sisters who are busier than ever in this season of life. Offer a helping hand. Remind them that they are doing a good job.

- Day 29 -

Blessed are the peacemakers, for they will be called children of God..

Matthew 5:9

Mamas, daughters, sisters, friends-we love peace between all of us, don't we? Our Savior does too! It's a worthy endeavor with beautiful rewards of mending and restoration. Those who ward off drama, or reconnect broken relationships are some of the silent heroes that walk among us!

Who needs to hear encouraging words to encourage restoration today? How can you pray for them? What inspiring words can you speak that will compel them to desire renewal and rebuilding in their broken situations?

- Day 30 -

Whenever the spirit from God came on Saul, David would take up his lyre and play. Then relief would come to Saul; he would feel better, and the evil spirit would leave him.

1 Samuel 16:23

Music plays a greater part in our lives than some people realize. Lyrics and tunes that are spiritually uplifting can transform our day! It can push away negative and evil spirits, while inviting our souls to embrace the beauty of our Lord all over again. It can make us rejoice, repent, find increased faith and more!

What inspirational songs have touched your heart this week? Did any particular part of the lyrics impact your current situations in life? What actions did they compel in your heart? Write it down.

- Day 31 -

But those who hope in the Lord will renew their strength. They will soar on wings like eagles; they will run and not grow weary, they will walk and not be faint.

Isaiah 40:31

Life has a way of making us tired. Physically, mentally, emotionally and spiritually. Even so, our remedy is to look to our Maker for our strength and refreshing. He holds the keys in His hand! Rest is at the tip of His fingers, if we spend some time with Him, share our cares, and let Him renew our strength once again.

What things do you find currently making you emotionally and spiritually tired? List them. Have you talked to Jesus about them? Make a note to share the heavy situations with Him today. Wait on Him. Let Him strengthen you.

- Day 32 -

Two are better than one, because they have a good return for their labor: If either of them falls down, one can help the other up. But pity anyone who falls and has no one to help them up..

Ecclesiastes 4:9-10

  Few gifts from God are as precious as a true friend. Companions for life! The Lord never intended for us to be islands all to ourselves. We're here to help each other!
The additional blessing in that? Lifting others has a way of lifting us as well! By word or deed, work to build each other up!

**Who needs to be lifted or helped today?
Write them down.
Pray for them. Pick up the phone and let them know they are on your heart at this moment.**

- Day 33 -

A gentle answer turns away wrath, but a harsh word stirs up anger.

Proverbs 15:1

Ladies, we have a tremendous weapon in our tone of voice and choice of words! We can say the most necessary statements of correction, and in return, witness remorse, humility and compliance-IF we offer gentleness. Nobody enjoys feeling attacked. The remedy is truth spoken in love.

Have you been putting off a necessary conversation about a serious matter? Pray about the situation. Ask God to soften the heart of the one you need to speak to. Then approach that person with love, reassuring her you are for her. Your true desire is a solution, not a title to be right.

- Day 34 -

If my people, who are called by my name, will humble themselves and pray and seek my face and turn from their wicked ways, then I will hear from heaven, and I will forgive their sin and will heal their land.

2 Chronicles 7:14

More than ever, healing is needed throughout the world! How do we experience the healing of our country? Our state? Our city? Our neighborhood? Even our home? It starts with me. I need to humble myself and pray. I need to seek the Lord and correct even my smallest ways that are not like God. I need to take care of me first.

Are there small things in your life you know are not pleasing to God? Write them down. Repent of them and pray for God's overcoming power to help you. As you focus on fixing your wrongs, begin having faith for your home, your neighborhood, and the world!

- Day 35 -

The one who gets wisdom loves life; the one who cherishes understanding will soon prosper.

Proverbs 19:8

How many of us have admired the wisdom of others we've had the privilege of knowing? Do we realize we can be counted among the wise too? Nuggets of learning can be found in nearly everything we see, touch, hear and experience. The requirement to make this happen is to simply pay attention. See how different things relate to the Word, to spiritual lessons. Be blessed!

Can you think of a few experiences that have taught you a spiritual lesson? What simple areas of life can you parallel with Biblical principles or teachings? Write it down.

- Day 36 -

Pride goes before destruction, a haughty spirit before a fall.

Proverbs 16:18

It's easy to get caught up in the glory of our accomplishments. Easy, but dangerous! Having confidence in our abilities is good, but we must never forget the Lord who gave us the ability to learn and do well. Not everyone is as fortunate as we are. Thankfulness is the attitude that prevents us from falling because of pride.

List your strong points, skills and talents. Do you ever struggle with pride because of any of them? It's a good time to examine your spirit and attitude to ensure they are what they should be. If they aren't, talk to the One who has blessed you. Let Him remind you of His goodness for your abilities.

- Day 37 -

*Give careful thought to the paths for your feet
and be steadfast in all your ways. Do not turn
to the right or the left; keep your foot from evil*

Proverbs 4:26-27

We're all faced with choices every day. Many
of them are decisions between doing what is
right and doing what is wrong. They apply
to both our physical and spiritual steps.
Thinking through our choices to the point of
the end results can save us from great
heartache and backslidings. We must not
choose the easy ways. We must choose the
right ways.

**What current situations need your
decisions? Walk through your possible end
results, depending on the choices you make.
Pray for the Lord to guide your steps. Let
Him speak to you through His Word, so that
your choices are made through wisdom.**

- Day 38 -

As iron sharpens iron, so one person sharpens another.

Proverbs 27:17

Having a relationship with Jesus births us into a grand family. The children of God are at various levels of learning and growing. Being in the Lord's family, it's only natural to talk about ur journey and all that we are learning. Let's take some time to share what we've studied and discovered. Let's join together to help each other know Him more!

What are some of your favorite topics to learn about in the Scriptures? Write them down. Locate and jot down related verses to study. Call a friend and ask them to join you.

- Day 39 -

The wise woman builds her house, but with her own hands the foolish one tears hers down.

Proverbs 14:1

Never-ending laundry, dishes and to-do lists tempt us to complain. We want others to sympathize with how hard we work. We want them to join our frustration as we grumble about our lazy children and sloppy husbands or inconsiderate roommates. Don't! Never give reason for others to look down on those we love. We're just tired. Let us be wise! Let us brag about their tender hearts and their own efforts at hard work instead.

What are some things you really appreciate about your family? Have you mentioned these things to them? After writing them down, take a few minutes to pray for them. Make a point today to tell each of them the specific things you appreciate about them.

- Day 40 -

Do everything in love.

1 Corinthians 16:14

Nothing is more beautiful than love. True love
has been given to us by the One who created us. It has further been proven through His sacrifice on the cross. His Spirit within radiates that love to the rest of the world. Love is a great conqueror. Love wins!

Who are you praying for that need to feel the love of God? Maybe even an extra dose? Pray for them and reach out! Remind them that they are loved–by God and by you!

A wife of noble character who can find?

She is worth far more than rubies.

Proverbs 31:10

Come to me, all you who are weary
and burdened, and I will give you rest.
Matthew 11:28

You shall be a crown of beauty
in the hand of the Lord
and a royal diadem in the hand of your God
Isa 62:3

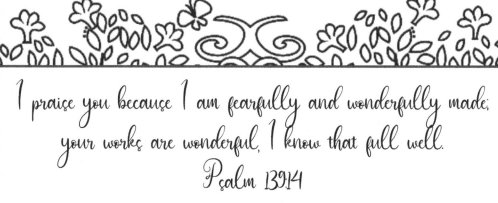

I praise you because I am fearfully and wonderfully made;
your works are wonderful, I know that full well.
Psalm 139:14